MAXIMIZING

THE

FREELANCE MARKET

DEDICATION

I dedicate this book all that want to create wealth in this digital age.

Establishing Your Brand as a Freelance Marketer 18

Crafting Your Personal Brand: 18

Creating a Compelling Marketing Message: 19

Leveraging Social Media and Networking Platforms: 19

Creating a Professional Online Presence: 20

Building a Reputation for Excellence: 20

CHAPTER 5

Finding and Attracting Clients 22

Strategies for Prospecting and Lead Generation: ... 22

Building Relationships with Potential Clients: 23

Pitching and Selling Your Services Effectively: 23

Utilizing Freelance Platforms and Job Boards: 24

Networking and Referrals: 24

CHAPTER 6

Delivering Exceptional Results 26

Setting Clear Expectations with Clients: 26

Managing Projects and Deadlines: 27

Providing Value-Added Services and Exceeding Client Expectations: 27

Maintaining Open and Transparent Communication: 28

Seeking Feedback and Continuous Improvement: 29

CONTENTS

DEDICATION **2**

CHAPTER 1
Introduction 7
   Overview of the Freelance Marketing Landscape: .. 7
   Importance of Freelancing in Today's Digital Economy: 8
   Brief History and Evolution of Freelance Marketing: 8

CHAPTER 2
   Understanding Freelance Marketing 10
   Definition and Scope of Freelance Marketing: 10
   Types of Freelance Marketing Services: 11
   Skills and Expertise Required for Success in Freelance Marketing: 12

CHAPTER 3
   Getting Started in Freelance Marketing 14
   Assessing Your Skills and Interests: 14
   Building a Portfolio and Online Presence: 15
   Finding Your Niche in the Market: 15
   Exploring Networking Opportunities: 16
   Investing in Continuous Learning: 16

CHAPTER 4

CHAPTER 7

Managing Finances and Negotiating Rates 30

Setting Freelance Rates and Pricing Strategies: 30

Budgeting and Managing Finances: 31

Invoicing and Payment Collection: 31

Negotiation Tactics for Securing Higher Rates: 32

Managing Scope Creep and Scope Changes: 32

CHAPTER 8

Scaling Your Freelance Marketing Business 34

Hirig Subcontractors or Building a Team: 34

Expanding Your Service Offerings: 35

Creating Systems for Efficiency and Growth: 35

Investing in Marketing and Branding: 36

Seeking Strategic Partnerships and Collaborations: 36

CHAPTER 9

Overcoming Challenges and Pitfalls 38

Dealing with Client Rejections and Setbacks: 38

Managing Burnout and Maintaining Work-Life Balance: 39

Adapting to Changes in the Market and Industry Trends: 39

Navigating Uncertainty and Financial Instability: 40

Coping with Isolation and Loneliness: 41

CHAPTER 10

Staying Relevant and Continuously Learning 42

The Importance of Ongoing Education and Skill Development: 42

Keeping Up with Advancements in Technology and Marketing Trends: 43

Building a Network of Peers and Mentors for Support and Learning: 44

Embracing Lifelong Learning as a Mindset: 44

Conclusion 46

CHAPTER 1

Introduction

In the rapidly evolving digital economy, freelance marketing has emerged as a pivotal force driving businesses' growth and success. This introduction sets the stage for understanding the dynamic world of freelance marketing, exploring its significance, evolution, and the opportunities it presents for individuals seeking independence and entrepreneurial fulfillment.

Overview of the Freelance Marketing Landscape:

Freelance marketing encompasses a broad spectrum of services aimed at helping businesses reach their target audience, increase brand visibility, and drive sales. From digital marketing to content creation, social media management, SEO, email marketing, and more, freelancers play a vital role in shaping modern marketing strategies.

Importance of Freelancing in Today's Digital Economy:

The rise of the gig economy and the increasing demand for flexible workforce solutions have propelled freelance marketing to the forefront of business operations. Companies of all sizes, from startups to multinational corporations, leverage the expertise of freelance marketers to access specialized skills, reduce overhead costs, and adapt to market dynamics swiftly.

Brief History and Evolution of Freelance Marketing:

While the concept of freelancing dates back centuries, the digital age has revolutionized the way freelance marketing operates. Historically, freelancers operated within local communities, relying on word-of-mouth referrals and traditional advertising channels. However, the advent of the internet and digital technologies has democratized access to freelance opportunities, enabling marketers to connect with clients globally and work remotely.

Today, freelance marketing is a thriving industry fueled by technological advancements, changing consumer behaviors, and the increasing importance of online presence for businesses. As the digital landscape continues to evolve, freelance marketers must adapt their strategies and skill sets to remain competitive and relevant in an ever-changing market.

In this book, we delve into the intricacies of freelance marketing, providing aspiring freelancers with the knowledge, tools, and strategies needed to navigate this dynamic field successfully. Whether you're a seasoned marketing professional looking to transition into freelancing or a newcomer eager to explore the possibilities, this comprehensive guide will equip you with the insights and resources to thrive in the freelance marketing landscape.

CHAPTER 2

Understanding Freelance Marketing

In this chapter, we delve deeper into the concept of freelance marketing, providing a comprehensive understanding of its scope, various service offerings, and the skills required to excel in this field. By gaining clarity on what freelance marketing entails, aspiring freelancers can better position themselves for success in the competitive market.

Definition and Scope of Freelance Marketing:

Freelance marketing encompasses a wide range of services aimed at promoting products, services, or brands on behalf of clients. This can include digital marketing, content creation, social media management, search engine optimization (SEO), email marketing, pay-per-click advertising, and more. Unlike traditional employment models, freelance marketers operate as independent contractors, offering their services to multiple clients on a project-by-project basis.

Types of Freelance Marketing Services:

Within the realm of freelance marketing, there are various specialized services that cater to different aspects of a client's marketing needs. These services may include:

Digital Marketing: Utilizing digital channels such as websites, social media, email, and search engines to reach and engage target audiences.

Content Creation: Developing high-quality written, visual, or multimedia content to inform, entertain, or persuade audiences.

Social Media Management: Managing and optimizing social media profiles, creating engaging content, and fostering community engagement.

SEO (Search Engine Optimization): Improving a website's visibility and ranking in search engine results pages (SERPs) through optimization techniques.

Email Marketing: Designing, executing, and analyzing email campaigns to nurture leads, retain customers, and drive conversions.

PPC (Pay-Per-Click) Advertising: Creating and managing paid advertising campaigns on platforms like Google Ads, Facebook Ads, and LinkedIn Ads to drive targeted traffic and generate leads.

Skills and Expertise Required for Success in Freelance Marketing:

To excel as a freelance marketer, individuals need a diverse skill set encompassing both technical and soft skills. These may include:

Marketing Strategy: Developing comprehensive marketing plans tailored to clients' goals and target audiences.

Communication Skills: Articulating ideas clearly, building rapport with clients, and effectively conveying value propositions.

Analytical Abilities: Interpreting data, tracking key performance indicators (KPIs), and optimizing marketing campaigns for maximum ROI.

Creativity: Generating innovative ideas, crafting compelling content, and devising unique strategies to capture audience attention.

Technical Proficiency: Familiarity with digital marketing tools, platforms, and analytics software to execute campaigns and measure results effectively.

Time Management: Prioritizing tasks, meeting deadlines, and managing multiple projects simultaneously in a fast-paced environment.

By understanding the breadth of freelance marketing services and honing the necessary skills, aspiring freelancers can position themselves as valuable assets to clients and embark on a rewarding career path in the dynamic world of freelance marketing.

CHAPTER 3

Getting Started in Freelance Marketing

Embarking on a career in freelance marketing requires careful planning, preparation, and strategic positioning to stand out in a competitive market. In this chapter, we explore the essential steps to help aspiring freelancers kickstart their journey and build a solid foundation for success.

Assessing Your Skills and Interests:

Before diving into freelance marketing, take time to evaluate your strengths, weaknesses, and areas of interest within the field. Reflect on your previous experiences, education, and skill set to identify your unique value proposition as a freelance marketer. Consider your passions, talents, and the types of projects you enjoy working on, as this will guide your niche selection and positioning in the market.

Building a Portfolio and Online Presence:

A compelling portfolio is essential for showcasing your expertise, demonstrating past successes, and attracting potential clients. Start by compiling examples of your work, including case studies, sample projects, and testimonials from satisfied clients or employers. Create a professional website or online portfolio where you can showcase your portfolio, highlight your services, and provide contact information for prospective clients.

Finding Your Niche in the Market:

Identifying a niche market or specialization is key to establishing yourself as a sought-after freelance marketer. Consider your unique skills, experiences, and interests, as well as market demand and competition, when selecting your niche. Whether it's social media marketing for small businesses, content creation for e-commerce brands, or SEO consulting for startups, specializing in a specific area allows you to position yourself as an expert and attract clients who value your expertise.

Exploring Networking Opportunities:

Networking plays a crucial role in the success of freelance marketers, providing opportunities for collaboration, referrals, and client acquisition. Join professional networking groups, attend industry events, and participate in online forums and communities relevant to your niche. Cultivate relationships with fellow freelancers, industry professionals, and potential clients to expand your network and increase your visibility in the freelance marketing community.

Investing in Continuous Learning:

The field of marketing is constantly evolving, with new trends, technologies, and strategies emerging regularly. Stay ahead of the curve by investing in continuous learning and professional development. Attend workshops, webinars, and conferences, enroll in online courses, and read industry publications to expand your knowledge, sharpen your skills, and stay updated on the latest trends and best practices in freelance marketing.

By taking proactive steps to assess your skills, build your portfolio, identify your niche, network with industry peers, and invest in continuous learning, you can lay the groundwork for a successful career in freelance marketing. With dedication, perseverance, and a strategic approach, you can turn your passion for marketing into a thriving freelance business.

CHAPTER 4

Establishing Your Brand as a Freelance Marketer

In the competitive landscape of freelance marketing, building a strong personal brand is essential for standing out, attracting clients, and fostering trust and credibility. This chapter explores the key elements of establishing a compelling brand identity as a freelance marketer and strategies for effectively communicating your value proposition to potential clients.

Crafting Your Personal Brand:

Your personal brand is a reflection of who you are, what you stand for, and the unique value you bring to the table as a freelance marketer. Start by defining your brand identity, including your core values, personality traits, and professional ethos. Consider how you want to be perceived by clients and colleagues and what sets you apart from other freelance marketers in your niche.

Creating a Compelling Marketing Message:

Once you've defined your brand identity, craft a clear and compelling marketing message that communicates your unique value proposition to potential clients. Your marketing message should succinctly articulate who you are, what you do, who you serve, and the benefits clients can expect from working with you. Focus on addressing the pain points and needs of your target audience and highlighting how your skills and expertise can help them achieve their goals.

Leveraging Social Media and Networking Platforms:

Social media and networking platforms offer powerful channels for building and promoting your personal brand as a freelance marketer. Choose platforms that align with your target audience and industry, whether it's LinkedIn for professional networking, Twitter for industry insights and thought leadership, or Instagram for visual storytelling and portfolio showcasing. Consistently share valuable content, engage with your audience, and participate in relevant conversations to increase your visibility and credibility as a freelance marketer.

Creating a Professional Online Presence:

In addition to social media, establish a professional online presence through your website, blog, or online portfolio. Invest in a professional website design that reflects your brand identity and showcases your portfolio, services, and client testimonials. Regularly update your blog or publish thought leadership articles to demonstrate your expertise and provide value to your audience. Optimize your online presence for search engines to improve your visibility and attract organic traffic from potential clients searching for freelance marketing services.

Building a Reputation for Excellence:

Delivering exceptional results and providing outstanding customer service are essential for building a reputation for excellence as a freelance marketer. Consistently exceed client expectations, communicate proactively, and deliver projects on time and within budget. Encourage satisfied clients to provide testimonials or referrals to strengthen your credibility and attract new business. By consistently delivering high-quality work and building positive relationships with clients, you can establish yourself as a trusted and reputable freelance marketer in your industry.

By focusing on crafting a compelling personal brand, communicating your value proposition effectively, leveraging social media and networking platforms, creating a professional online presence, and building a reputation for excellence, you can establish yourself as a standout freelance marketer and attract clients who recognize and appreciate the unique value you bring to the table.

CHAPTER 5

Finding and Attracting Clients

Securing clients is essential for sustaining a successful freelance marketing business. In this chapter, we explore effective strategies for identifying, reaching out to, and attracting potential clients who are in need of your services.

Strategies for Prospecting and Lead Generation:

Prospecting involves identifying and qualifying potential clients who are likely to benefit from your freelance marketing services. Start by defining your ideal client profile based on factors such as industry, company size, target audience, and marketing needs. Utilize online tools and databases to research potential clients, such as business directories, LinkedIn, and industry-specific forums. Tailor your outreach efforts to each prospect, highlighting how your services can address their specific pain points and help them achieve their business goals.

Maximizing the Freelance Market

Building Relationships with Potential Clients:

Building genuine relationships with potential clients is key to earning their trust and ultimately securing their business. Engage with prospects on social media, comment on their posts, and share valuable insights relevant to their industry or niche. Attend industry events, webinars, and networking mixers to connect with potential clients in person and establish rapport. Offer to provide value upfront, such as a free consultation or audit, to demonstrate your expertise and build credibility.

Pitching and Selling Your Services Effectively:

Crafting a compelling pitch is essential for persuading potential clients to hire you for their marketing needs. Tailor your pitch to each prospect, focusing on how your services can solve their specific challenges and deliver tangible results. Highlight your unique selling points, past successes, and relevant experience to differentiate yourself from competitors. Be confident, concise, and persuasive in your pitch, and always follow up with prospects to address any questions or concerns they may have.

Utilizing Freelance Platforms and Job Boards:

Freelance platforms and job boards can be valuable resources for finding freelance marketing opportunities and connecting with clients in need of your services. Create a profile on popular freelance platforms such as Upwork, Freelancer, and Fiverr, and actively search for relevant projects that match your skills and expertise. Customize your profile to showcase your portfolio, highlight your qualifications, and include client testimonials to attract potential clients browsing the platform.

Networking and Referrals:

Networking remains one of the most effective ways to find and attract clients as a freelance marketer. Leverage your existing network of colleagues, friends, and industry contacts to generate referrals and introductions to potential clients. Attend industry events, join professional associations, and participate in online forums and communities to expand your network and increase your visibility within your target market. Nurture relationships with existing clients and ask for referrals or testimonials to help you attract new business through word-of-mouth recommendations.

By implementing a combination of proactive prospecting, relationship-building, effective pitching, leveraging freelance platforms, and networking, you can effectively find and attract clients who are in need of your freelance marketing services. Stay persistent, adapt your approach based on feedback and results, and continuously refine your strategies to maximize your success in attracting and securing new clients.

CHAPTER 6

Delivering Exceptional Results

Once you've successfully attracted clients, delivering exceptional results is crucial for maintaining long-term relationships, earning repeat business, and building a positive reputation as a freelance marketer. In this chapter, we explore strategies for setting clear expectations, managing projects efficiently, and exceeding client expectations to ensure client satisfaction and success.

Setting Clear Expectations with Clients:

Clear communication and expectation setting are paramount to the success of any client engagement. From the outset, establish clear objectives, timelines, deliverables, and budget parameters with your clients. Ensure that both parties have a mutual understanding of the project scope, goals, and any potential challenges or constraints. Document all agreements and expectations in a written contract or statement of work to minimize misunderstandings and disputes down the line.

Managing Projects and Deadlines:

Effective project management is essential for delivering projects on time and within budget while maintaining quality standards. Break down larger projects into manageable tasks, set realistic deadlines for each task, and prioritize your workload based on urgency and importance. Utilize project management tools and software to track progress, communicate with clients, and collaborate with team members if applicable. Regularly update clients on project status, milestones achieved, and any changes or deviations from the original plan.

Providing Value-Added Services and Exceeding Client Expectations:

Going above and beyond to exceed client expectations is a surefire way to earn their trust, loyalty, and future business. Look for opportunities to provide value-added services or insights that enhance the overall impact of your work. Offer strategic recommendations, creative ideas, or additional resources that demonstrate your commitment to achieving the client's objectives. Anticipate their needs, proactively address any challenges or concerns, and consistently deliver results that exceed their expectations.

Maintaining Open and Transparent Communication:

Effective communication is the cornerstone of successful client relationships. Keep clients informed and involved throughout the project lifecycle, providing regular updates, progress reports, and opportunities for feedback. Be responsive to client inquiries, questions, and feedback, and address any concerns or issues promptly and professionally. Establishing a communication cadence and preferred channels of communication early on can help streamline communication and ensure alignment between you and your clients.

Seeking Feedback and Continuous Improvement:

Feedback is invaluable for learning and growth as a freelance marketer. Encourage clients to provide honest feedback on your work, communication style, and overall client experience. Use feedback as an opportunity to identify areas for improvement, refine your processes, and enhance the quality of your services. Continuously seek opportunities for learning and professional development to stay ahead of industry trends, expand your skill set, and deliver even better results for your clients.

By setting clear expectations, managing projects efficiently, providing value-added services, maintaining open communication, and seeking feedback for continuous improvement, you can consistently deliver exceptional results that delight your clients and differentiate you as a top-notch freelance marketer in the industry.

CHAPTER 7

Managing Finances and Negotiating Rates

Managing finances effectively and negotiating competitive rates are essential aspects of running a successful freelance marketing business. In this chapter, we explore strategies for setting freelance rates, budgeting, invoicing, and negotiating contracts to ensure financial stability and profitability.

Setting Freelance Rates and Pricing Strategies:

Determining your freelance rates requires careful consideration of factors such as your level of expertise, market demand, industry benchmarks, and the value you provide to clients. Research prevailing rates for freelance marketing services in your niche and geographic location to establish a competitive pricing structure. Consider your overhead costs, desired income, and profit margins when setting your rates. You may choose to bill clients hourly, project-based, or on a retainer basis, depending on the nature of the project and your preferences.

Budgeting and Managing Finances:

As a freelance marketer, it's essential to manage your finances effectively to ensure a steady income and financial stability. Create a detailed budget outlining your monthly expenses, including business-related costs such as software subscriptions, marketing expenses, and professional development. Set aside funds for taxes, retirement savings, and emergency expenses. Use accounting software or spreadsheets to track income and expenses, monitor cash flow, and maintain accurate financial records for tax purposes.

Invoicing and Payment Collection:

Establish clear invoicing and payment terms with your clients to streamline the billing process and ensure timely payment. Create professional invoices detailing the services rendered, rates, payment due dates, and accepted payment methods. Send invoices promptly upon project completion or according to the agreed-upon billing schedule. Follow up with clients who are overdue on payments, and implement late payment penalties or incentives to encourage prompt payment. Consider using online invoicing platforms or payment processing services to automate invoicing and facilitate payment collection.

Negotiation Tactics for Securing Higher Rates:

Negotiating rates effectively is essential for maximizing your earning potential as a freelance marketer. Prepare thoroughly for negotiations by researching market rates, understanding the client's budget constraints, and highlighting the value you bring to the table. Focus on articulating the benefits and outcomes of your services rather than justifying your rates based on time or effort. Be confident, assertive, and prepared to walk away from negotiations that do not align with your financial goals or value proposition.

Managing Scope Creep and Scope Changes:

Scope creep, or the gradual expansion of project scope beyond the original agreement, can have a significant impact on your time, resources, and profitability as a freelance marketer. Mitigate scope creep by clearly defining project scope, deliverables, and timeline in the initial contract or statement of work. Establish a formal change management process for handling scope changes, including how additional work will be billed and approved. Communicate proactively with clients about any changes or deviations from the original scope to ensure alignment and avoid misunderstandings.

By implementing effective strategies for setting freelance rates, managing finances, invoicing, negotiating contracts, and mitigating scope creep, you can ensure financial stability and profitability in your freelance marketing business. Stay proactive, informed, and strategic in your approach to financial management, and continually evaluate and adjust your pricing and billing practices to optimize your earning potential and business success.

CHAPTER 8

Scaling Your Freelance Marketing Business

Scaling your freelance marketing business involves expanding your capacity, increasing your revenue streams, and taking strategic steps to grow your client base and service offerings. In this chapter, we explore strategies for scaling your freelance marketing business sustainably and strategically.

Hirig Subcontractors or Building a Team:

As your workload increases and your business grows, consider hiring subcontractors or building a team to help you manage projects and serve clients more efficiently. Identify talented freelancers or professionals with complementary skills who can support your business needs. Establish clear expectations, roles, and communication channels with your team members, and provide ongoing support and feedback to ensure success. Delegating tasks and collaborating with a team can help you take on larger projects, expand your capacity, and deliver exceptional results to clients.

Expanding Your Service Offerings:

Diversifying your service offerings can open up new revenue streams and attract clients with varying needs and preferences. Evaluate your skills, expertise, and market demand to identify potential areas for expansion. Consider offering additional services such as consulting, coaching, training workshops, or package deals that bundle multiple services together. Keep abreast of industry trends, emerging technologies, and client demands to stay relevant and competitive in the market.

Creating Systems for Efficiency and Growth:

Developing efficient systems and processes is crucial for scaling your freelance marketing business while maintaining quality and consistency. Implement project management tools, automation software, and workflow systems to streamline your operations, improve productivity, and reduce manual tasks. Standardize your workflows, templates, and communication protocols to ensure consistency and minimize errors. Continuously evaluate and refine your systems to adapt to changing business needs and optimize efficiency.

Investing in Marketing and Branding:

Investing in marketing and branding efforts can help you increase your visibility, attract new clients, and position your business for growth. Develop a comprehensive marketing strategy that includes a mix of online and offline tactics such as content marketing, social media advertising, email campaigns, networking events, and industry partnerships. Consistently promote your brand message, showcase your expertise, and demonstrate the value you provide to clients to differentiate yourself in the market and attract high-quality leads.

Seeking Strategic Partnerships and Collaborations:

Forming strategic partnerships and collaborations with complementary businesses or professionals can expand your reach, access new markets, and create opportunities for mutual growth. Identify potential partners who share your target audience or offer complementary services that enhance your own offerings. Explore joint marketing initiatives, referral programs, or co-branded projects that leverage each other's strengths and resources. Collaborating with strategic partners can help you tap into new opportunities, expand your client base, and achieve your business goals more effectively.

By adopting strategic approaches such as hiring subcontractors, expanding service offerings, creating efficient systems, investing in marketing, and seeking strategic partnerships, you can scale your freelance marketing business effectively while maintaining quality and client satisfaction. Stay agile, adaptable, and proactive in your approach to growth, and continually assess and adjust your strategies to align with your business objectives and market dynamics.

CHAPTER 9

Overcoming Challenges and Pitfalls

While freelancing offers numerous benefits, it also comes with its own set of challenges and pitfalls. In this chapter, we explore common obstacles that freelance marketers may encounter and strategies for overcoming them to achieve long-term success and fulfillment in their careers.

Dealing with Client Rejections and Setbacks:

Rejection and setbacks are inevitable parts of the freelancing journey. Clients may reject proposals, projects may not go as planned, or you may encounter unforeseen challenges along the way. To overcome client rejections and setbacks, maintain a positive mindset and resilience in the face of adversity. Learn from each experience, identify areas for improvement, and use feedback constructively to refine your approach. Remember that setbacks are opportunities for growth and development, and every rejection brings you one step closer to success.

Managing Burnout and Maintaining Work-Life Balance:

Freelance marketers often juggle multiple projects, deadlines, and client demands, which can lead to burnout and overwhelm if not managed effectively. Prioritize self-care and establish boundaries to maintain a healthy work-life balance. Schedule regular breaks, set realistic expectations for your workload, and learn to say no to projects or clients that don't align with your priorities or values. Delegate tasks, outsource non-core activities, and seek support from peers, mentors, or mental health professionals if needed. Remember that your well-being is paramount to your long-term success as a freelancer.

Adapting to Changes in the Market and Industry Trends:

The marketing landscape is constantly evolving, with new technologies, trends, and consumer behaviors shaping the industry. Freelance marketers must stay agile and adaptable to remain relevant in a rapidly changing market. Invest in continuous learning and professional development to keep abreast of industry trends, emerging technologies, and best practices. Adapt your skills and service offerings to meet evolving client needs and market demands. Embrace change as an opportunity for growth and innovation, and be proactive in anticipating and responding to shifts in the market.

Navigating Uncertainty and Financial Instability:

Freelancing inherently involves a degree of financial uncertainty, as income may fluctuate from month to month depending on project availability and client demand. To navigate financial instability, practice prudent financial management and budgeting. Build an emergency fund to cover unexpected expenses or periods of low income. Diversify your client base and revenue streams to mitigate risk and increase stability. Consider taking on retainer clients or long-term contracts to provide a more predictable income stream. Stay proactive in seeking new opportunities, marketing your services, and expanding your network to ensure a steady flow of work.

Coping with Isolation and Loneliness:

Freelancing can be isolating, especially for those who work remotely or independently. Combat feelings of loneliness by actively seeking out opportunities for connection and community. Join freelance networks, online forums, or coworking spaces where you can connect with like-minded professionals, share experiences, and seek support. Attend industry events, conferences, or meetups to network with peers and expand your social circle. Cultivate relationships with fellow freelancers, mentors, or industry associations to foster a sense of belonging and camaraderie in your freelance journey.

By acknowledging and addressing common challenges such as client rejections, burnout, market changes, financial instability, and isolation, freelance marketers can develop resilience, adaptability, and strategies for overcoming obstacles in their careers. Stay proactive, resourceful, and open to learning and growth as you navigate the ups and downs of the freelancing journey.

CHAPTER 10

Staying Relevant and Continuously Learning

In the dynamic field of freelance marketing, staying relevant and continuously learning are essential for maintaining a competitive edge, adapting to industry changes, and maximizing career growth opportunities. In this chapter, we explore strategies for ongoing education, skill development, and networking to ensure long-term success and relevance as a freelance marketer.

The Importance of Ongoing Education and Skill Development:

The marketing landscape is constantly evolving, with new technologies, platforms, and strategies emerging regularly. To stay ahead of the curve, prioritize ongoing education and skill development. Invest in relevant courses, workshops, and certifications to expand your knowledge and expertise in areas such as digital marketing, data analytics, content creation, and emerging technologies. Stay informed about industry trends, best practices, and case studies through industry publications, blogs, podcasts, and webinars. Continuously seek opportunities to learn, experiment, and refine your skills to remain competitive in the ever-changing market.

Keeping Up with Advancements in Technology and Marketing Trends:

Technology plays a pivotal role in shaping the future of marketing, with innovations such as artificial intelligence, machine learning, augmented reality, and voice search revolutionizing the way businesses connect with their audiences. Stay abreast of advancements in technology and marketing trends to leverage new opportunities and stay ahead of the competition. Experiment with emerging tools and platforms, such as AI-powered chatbots, predictive analytics software, or virtual reality experiences, to enhance your marketing strategies and deliver innovative solutions to clients. Embrace a mindset of curiosity and adaptability, and be open to exploring new technologies and trends that can propel your freelance marketing career forward.

Building a Network of Peers and Mentors for Support and Learning:

Networking is a valuable resource for freelance marketers, providing opportunities for collaboration, mentorship, and professional growth. Cultivate relationships with peers, mentors, and industry experts who can offer guidance, feedback, and support throughout your freelance journey. Join professional associations, attend industry events, and participate in online communities and forums to expand your network and connect with like-minded professionals. Seek out mentors who have achieved success in your desired niche or field and learn from their experiences, insights, and best practices. Actively engage with your network, offer value, and be willing to reciprocate support and assistance to foster mutually beneficial relationships.

Embracing Lifelong Learning as a Mindset:

Lifelong learning is not just about acquiring new skills or knowledge—it's a mindset and a commitment to personal and professional growth. Approach your freelance marketing career with a growth mindset, embracing challenges, setbacks, and opportunities as learning experiences. Stay curious, adaptable, and proactive in seeking out new learning opportunities, whether it's through formal education, hands-on experimentation, or peer collaboration. View failure as a stepping stone to success, and use feedback and setbacks as opportunities for reflection and improvement. By adopting a lifelong learning mindset, you can continuously evolve, innovate, and thrive in the ever-changing landscape of freelance marketing.

In summary, staying relevant and continuously learning are essential for success and longevity in the freelance marketing industry. Prioritize ongoing education, stay informed about advancements in technology and marketing trends, build a network of peers and mentors for support and learning, and embrace lifelong learning as a mindset to ensure your continued growth and success as a freelance marketer.

Conclusion

Congratulations on reaching the end of "Freelance Marketing: Navigating the Digital Landscape for Success"! Throughout this book, we've explored the dynamic world of freelance marketing, providing comprehensive insights, strategies, and resources to help you thrive in this competitive and ever-evolving industry.

As you embark on your freelance marketing journey, remember that success is not just about talent or luck—it's about dedication, resilience, and continuous learning. Whether you're a seasoned marketer looking to transition into freelancing or a newcomer eager to explore the possibilities, the principles and strategies outlined in this book can serve as your roadmap to success.

From understanding the fundamentals of freelance marketing and finding your niche to attracting clients, delivering exceptional results, and scaling your business, each chapter has equipped you with the knowledge, tools, and strategies needed to build a thriving freelance marketing career.

As you apply these insights and strategies to your freelance business, remember to stay proactive, adaptable, and committed to your growth and development. Embrace challenges as opportunities for learning and growth, cultivate strong relationships with clients and peers, and always strive for excellence in everything you do.

Finally, remember that success in freelance marketing is not just about financial gain—it's about finding fulfillment, autonomy, and purpose in your work. Stay true to your values, passions, and goals, and let them guide you on your journey to success as a freelance marketer.

Thank you for joining us on this journey through the world of freelance marketing. Here's to your continued growth, success, and fulfillment as a freelance marketer!

www.ingramcontent.com/pod-product-compliance
Lightning Source LLC
Chambersburg PA
CBHW030057230526
45471CB00003B/1130